D0887112

SIMPLICITY

AS

EVIDENCE OF TRUTH

The Aquinas Lecture, 1997

SIMPLICITY
AS
EVIDENCE OF TRUTH

Under the auspices of the
Wisconsin-Alpha Chapter of Phi Sigma Tau

by

RICHARD SWINBURNE

MARQUETTE
UNIVERSITY
PRESS

Library of Congress Cataloging-in-Publication Data

Swinburne, Richard.
    Simplicity as evidence of truth / by Richard Swinburne.
        p. cm. — (The Aquinas lecture ; 1997)
    "Under the auspices of the Wisconsin-Alpha Chapter of
Phi Sigma Tau."
    Includes bibliographical references.
    ISBN 0-87462-164-X (cloth)
    1. Explanation. 2. Simplicity (Philosophy) I. Title.
II. Series.
BD237.S85 1997
121'.6—dc21   96-51315

© 1997 Marquette University Press
Printed in the United States of America

MARQUETTE UNIVERSITY PRESS
MILWAUKEE

The Association of Jesuit University Presses

Prefatory

The Wisconsin-Alpha Chapter of Phi Sigma Tau, the International Honor Society for Philosophy at Marquette University, each year invites a scholar to deliver a lecture in honor of St. Thomas Aquinas.

The 1997 Aquinas Lecture, *Simplicity As Evidence of Truth,* was delivered in the Tony and Lucille Weasler Auditorium on Sunday, March 2, 1997, by Richard G. Swinburne, the Nolloth Professor of the Philosophy of the Christian Religion at the University of Oxford.

Professor Swinburne was educated at the University of Oxford where as an undergraduate he read for a B.A. in Philosophy, Politics, and Economics, which he received in 1957. He subsequently read for a B.Phil. in Philosophy, which he received in 1959 and for the Oxford Diploma in Theology, which he received in 1960. He was the Leverhulme Research Fellow in the History and Philosophy of Science at the University of Leeds (1961-1963). He was Lecturer in Philosophy at the University of Hull (1963-1972), Visiting Associate Professor of Philosophy at the University of Maryland (1969-1970), and Professor of Philosophy at the University of Keele (1972-1984). Since 1985 he has been the Nolloth Professor of the Philosophy of the Christian Religion at the University of Oxford. He was elected a Fellow of the British Academy in 1992.

Professor Swinburne has written *Space and Time* (1968), *The Concept of Miracle* (1971), *An Introduction to Confirmation Theory* (1973), a trilogy on the philosophy of theism: *The Coherence of Theism* (1977), *The Existence of God* (1979), and *Faith and Reason* (1981), *The Evolution of the Soul* (1986), three volumes of a projected tetralogy on the philosophy of Christian doctrine: *Responsibility and Atonement* (1989), *Revelation: From Metaphor to Analogy* (1991), and *The Christian God* (1994), in addition to *Is There a God?* (1996). He has also edited the following books: *The Justification of Induction* (1974), *Space, Time and Causality* (1983), and *Miracles* (1989), and is coauthor with Sydney Shoemaker of *Personal Identity* (1984). In 1994 Professor Swinburne was honored by many of his distinguished colleagues with a festschrift entitled: *Reason and the Christian Religion,* to which he contributed an essay, "Intellectual Autobiography." Among his more than seventy-five scholarly articles are "The Argument from the Fine-Tuning of the Universe," "Analytic/Synthetic," "Thisness," "Tensed Facts," "The Objectivity of Morality," "Necessary A Posteriori Truth," "God and Time," "The Beginning of Time and of the Universe."

To Professor Swinburne's distinguished list of publications, Phi Sigma Tau is pleased to add: *Simplicity As Evidence of Truth.*

SIMPLICITY
AS
EVIDENCE OF TRUTH

by

RICHARD SWINBURNE

SIMPLICITY
AS
EVIDENCE OF TRUTH

I seek in this essay to show that—other things being equal—the simplest hypothesis proposed as an explanation of phenomena is more likely to be the true one than is any other available hypothesis, that its predictions are more likely to be true than are those of any other available hypothesis, and that it is an ultimate a priori epistemic principle that simplicity is evidence of truth.

I. The Structure of Explanation

Before arguing my main contentions, I need to make a number of (mostly) very familiar points about the nature of explanation. Talk of explanation in this essay is talk of causal explanation, talk of the factors operative in bringing about some event. 'Explanation' and cognate words can be used in strong or weak senses. In a strong sense an explanation of an event is a true explanation, a description of factors which made the event occur. In a weak sense an explanation is a purported explanation in the strong sense, someone's suggestion for what might be a true explanation. I shall use 'explanation' in the strong sense; and instead of 'explanation' in the weak sense, talk of 'purported explanation.'

I suggest that there are two basic patterns of explanation—inanimate explanation, characteristic of the physical sciences and of much ordinary-life explanation, and personal explanation, characteristic of history and psychology and also of much other ordinary-life explanation.[1] In explanations of both kinds a phenomenon, that is, the occurrence of an event, is explained by a cause (or causes) and some principle (or principles) in virtue of which the cause (in the conditions then operative) brought about the event as effect. In the empiricist tradition of philosophy developed from Hume, the components of inanimate explanation are initial conditions, one of which we may designate in a somewhat arbitrary way as the cause, which we contrast with the conditions under which the cause operated, and regularities of succession, whereby events of one kind are always (or usually) followed by events of another kind. Thus the explanation of why a certain barrel of gunpowder exploded on a certain occasion is that it was caused by the gunpowder being ignited at a temperature and pressure within certain ranges in the presence of oxygen, and the by regularity that all gunpowder ignited in similar circumstances explodes. Whether one distinguishes between the ignition of the gunpowder as cause and the presence of oxygen, etc., as conditions necessary for the operation of the cause, or whether one draws the cause/ condition distinction in a different place is arbitrary.

It was soon recognized that in order to provide explanation, the regularities had to be lawlike. By the regularity's being lawlike I mean two things. First, it must license counterfactuals, that is, have consequences for what would happen or would have happened in unrealized circumstances. "All the National Lottery draws this month included a 31 among the numbers drawn" is a mere accidental regularity, because it does not license any counterfactual such as "If there had been another lottery draw this month, it would have produced a 31." (It does not license it either by entailing it or by making it more probable.) By contrast, "all metals expand when heated" does license the counterfactual that some other metal which was not heated would have expanded if it had been heated. Regularities which do not license counterfactuals (whether ones concerned with a narrow spatio-temporal region, or ones which hold far more widely) I will call accidental regularities. An accidental regularity can only be known through knowledge of all its instances. My only grounds for believing that all lottery draws this month included a 31 is by watching or reading the results of each of the draws. For if I had other grounds, if observation of some of the draws gave me grounds for a belief about the results of other draws, that would be because those grounds gave me reason to suppose that there was some propensity in the set-up to produce 31's. In that case I would have grounds for supposing that if there had been another draw, it too would have included a 31. And in that case the regularity would not have been accidental.

Second, in order to be lawlike, the regularity must not itself be derivable from regularities which connect events of the kind described in the former by chains of temporally contiguous events with a common initial condition, when there is no regularity connecting them by a more direct chain. The regularity R "Most falls of the barometer are followed by rain a day later" satisfies the first condition of licensing counterfactuals—if the barometer had fallen yesterday, it would have rained today. But R is derivable from two other regularities—"almost all falls of air pressure are followed by rain" and "almost all barometer falls are preceded by falls of air pressure." These two regularities can themselves be spelled out in terms of chains of regularly connected and temporally contiguous events from the falls of air pressure both to barometer falls and to rain, but there are no such direct chains from barometer falls to rain. For this reason, the barometer fall is no part of the explanation of the rain. A regularity which satisfies the first but not the second condition I will call an acausal regularity. Regularities which satisfy both conditions are lawlike. Though perhaps only the grandest of them normally get called laws of nature, I shall call them all laws of nature.

Laws may be of universal form—"all events of type A are followed by events of type B," and so in virtue of their counterfactual consequences are to be read

as "all events of type A of physical necessity are followed by events of type B." Or they may be of statistical form—"n% events of type A are followed by
events of type B," and so in virtue of their counterfactual consequences are to be read as "all events of
type A have a probability (that is, propensity) of
degree n/100 to be followed by events of type B."

The laws involved in an explanation of an event
may all be of universal form, and the statement
thereof together with a description of initial conditions may entail the event to be explained, and in
that case you have deductive-nomological explanation; or one or more of the laws may be statistical
and the description of those together with the description of the initial conditions render the
explanandum event (inductively) more probable
than it would otherwise be—and in that case you
have statistical-relevance explanation.[2]

Some philosophers, including myself, believe that
a substances-powers-and-liabilities (SPL) account of
inanimate explanation rather than a laws-and-ini-
tial conditions (LIC) account provides the meta-
physically correct account of inanimate explanation.
On this account[3] the cause or causes are not events
but the substances of which the events are states—
not the ignition of the gunpowder, but the gunpowder itself. The substances have causal powers, including a power to bring about an effect of the kind
of the event being explained, and liabilities to exercise those powers (a liability to exercise them inevi-
tably, or a probabilistically measurable propensity

to do so) under circumstances such as those in which
the event being explained occurred. The gunpowder has the power to produce an explosion and the
liability to exercise that power when ignited under
certain conditions of temperature and pressure in
the presence of oxygen, conditions which were mani-
fested at the relevant time; and so in virtue of its
powers and liabilities the gunpowder caused the explosion. Substances of the same kind have similar
powers and liabilities, and statements of the "laws
of nature" are simply statements to the effect that
substances of certain kinds have certain powers and
liabilities to use them under certain conditions. The
"law of nature" that all metals expand when heated
is just the regularity that all metals have the power
to expand and the liability to exercise it when heated.
Laws of nature are not then themselves causally ef-
ficacious factors; they are just contingent regularities in the causal powers and liabilities of substances.
Substances belong to the kinds they do in part because of the powers and liabilities they have. Some
liquid is an acid in part because it has the power to
turn litmus paper red and the liability to exercise
that power when the paper is put into the liquid.
The necessity or propensity in nature which gives
rise to counterfactuals arises, on the SPL account,
from the powers and liabilities of substances rather
than from laws of nature.

Explanation in terms of laws and initial conditions can easily be translated into explanation in
terms of substances, powers and liabilities, and vice-

versa, and nothing turns, for the main purposes of this essay, on which account we adopt. For ease of exposition, I shall use the more familiar laws-of-nature account.

In a personal explanation of some phenomena, it is persons (or other animate beings) who are the causes, and the principles in virtue of which they cause include their powers (to act intentionally), beliefs and desires. Its pattern is similar to that of inanimate explanation on the SPL model—except that liabilities to act, to use powers, arise from beliefs and desires and that the powers of persons are powers to bring about effects intentionally, that is, because they mean to do so. Whether they exercise some power will depend on their beliefs about the effects of doing so, their desires to bring about or not bring about this or that effect, and their beliefs about whether or not it would be a good thing to do so. The explanation of why my hand moved on some occasion is that I (the cause) intentionally made it move and that I did so because I have the power to make it move intentionally (that is, if I choose to) and because I believed that thereby I could catch someone's attention and that I desired or believed it good to catch their attention.[4]

A full explanation of some phenomenon is provided when the principles entail that the cause will bring about the effect, partial explanation when they make it more probable than otherwise that it will. For inanimate things, on one (and I believe the correct) interpretation of Quantum Theory, liabilities are only probabilistic propensities. Likewise I believe that human beings have free will, so that knowledge of their powers, desires and beliefs will not always enable you to deduce what they will bring about intentionally—so here too there will be only a partial explanation of effects.

Explanation may be deep or superficial. It is superficial in so far as the principles invoked are limited ones operative only in a narrow range of circumstances, their operation under those circumstances being explicable by a deeper principle. Lower-level laws (such as Kepler's laws) are (approximately) derivable (for relevant circumstances—that is, for massive bodies with the kinds of masses, distances apart and initial velocities of the sun and planets) from higher-level laws (such as Newton's laws) and the derivation may be deductive or inductive. Higher-level laws have more content (that is, carry consequences for far more kinds of phenomena than do lower-level laws), and often fit together into an overall theory. Higher-level laws provide deeper, more fundamental explanations of events, and the highest-level laws of all provide the most fundamental explanation. Likewise some piece of human behaviour may be explained by the agent's most immediate desire—my going to the door is explained by my desire to go to the kitchen, together with my belief that the kitchen lies through the door, but this desire is in turn explained by my desire for food together with my belief that there is food in the kitchen. The current motion of my hand is explained by my desire to write this sentence, but this in turn is explained by my desire to write the lecture and my belief that this sentence will contribute towards that.

II. Explanation and Prediction

Knowledge of the explanation of some event always gives one some ability to predict with justification further events (and likewise to retrodict events.[5] What I have to say here about prediction will—with minor changes—apply also to retrodiction, but for reasons of space, I will not discuss that further.) Knowledge of laws which explain some phenomenon enables one to predict further instances of their operation. If I know the explanation of the angle of refraction of a particular ray of light in terms of Snell's law, that allows me to predict the angle of refraction of another ray. If I know the beliefs and desires which led some person to do what he did, they will enable me to predict other actions he might perform.

The counter-examples which might naturally be adduced against the claim that knowledge of explanation makes possible prediction turn out to be cases when the explanation is only partial, and any resulting prediction has only a highly probabilistic character. Suppose you can catch malaria from contact with the malaria fly and in no other way. Then, it is said, if you catch malaria, I can know what explained this—you had contact with a malaria fly.

But that, it may be said, may not enable me to predict anything—for maybe only 1% of those in contact with the malaria fly catch malaria. But the response to this example is that the explanation is a very partial one—since your contact with the fly gave you a 1% chance of catching malaria, there is a lot more to be explained about why you caught it on this occasion. And yet, to the extent to which I know the explanation, I can predict with justification—I can predict (with probability well over 1/2) that if one hundred other people come in contact with the malaria fly, at least one of them will also catch malaria—which they would not do otherwise.

On the other hand, justified prediction is possible without knowledge of any explanation. I can note regularities, the uniformity of which gives me good reason to suppose that they are not accidental and which I have good reason to suppose are not lawlike; they are, I may believe with justification, acausal. I note that barometer falls are normally followed by rain and that enables me to predict rain—but I may not have the slightest idea of the explanation either of why the barometer falls or of what causes rain. In the absence of explanation, we rely for prediction on acausal regularities. When I learn the explanations, the factors involved there enable me to see the limits to the operation of the acausal regularity. When I learn what causes rain and how far those factors alone always cause barometer falls, I learn the limits to the extent to which falls of the barometer are indicative of rain.

I shall be suggesting that where our background knowledge indicates that some correlation between events of certain kinds is acausal rather than law-like, (namely, it indicates that events of the two kinds are likely to have a common cause which explains the correlation), we still regard the simplest hypothesis about the nature of the correlation as—other things being equal—that most likely to be true. Presumably this is because—other things being equal—we regard the simplest hypothesis connecting each kind of event with a prior common cause-event to be that most likely to be true, and so more likely to give rise to a simple acausal regularity rather than a complex one. But I shall mention such a case only *en passant*; my main concern will be with our choice between competing explanatory hypotheses and the predictions which they make possible.

III. The Best Explanation

Such is the nature of explanation and the power to predict that knowledge of explanation provides. But what are the criteria for supposing that some purported explanation, some one explanatory hypothesis rather than some other one provides the true explanation. There are, I am going to suggest, two a posteriori and two a priori criteria for determining this. These criteria have to be fairly well satisfied as a whole in order for us to be justified in supposing that we have an explanation at all. But, given that, then among incompatible purported

explanations the one which satisfies the criteria best
on the whole is the one which is most probably true.
It provides, in the weak sense of explanation, the
best explanation. On the a posteriori side there is,
first, the criterion of yielding the data, that is, leading us to expect the events to be explained—either
with deductive certainty or with inductive probability. The more data and the more probable some
hypothesis renders their occurrence, the more likely
it is that—that is, the more probable it is that—
that hypothesis is true.

Also, on the a posteriori side, a hypothesis needs
to fit in with our background knowledge, with everything else we know about the world, or rather it
is more likely to be true in so far as it does. The
hypothesis that John stole the money is rendered
more probable if we know that John has stolen on
other occasions or comes from a social group among
whom stealing is widespread. And if we do not know
but have some reason to believe these latter things,
to that lesser extent the probability of our hypothesis is increased. I shall shortly be arguing that the
notion of "fit" itself involves the crucial a priori factor of simplicity.

On the a priori side, there is, first, content. The
greater the content of a hypothesis the less it is likely
to be true. The more claims you make, the greater
the probability that your claims will contain some
falsity, and so be as a whole false. The content of a
hypothesis is a matter of how much it tells us about
the world—whether it tells us just about our planet,

or about all the planets of the solar system, or about all the planets in the universe; or whether it predicts exact values of many variables or only approximate values of few variables. There is no precise way of measuring content, but we can compare content. If one hypothesis entails another but is not entailed by it, the former has more content than the latter. And rough comparisons are possible between theories not thus logically related. A hypothesis which predicted all the positions of Mars for the next century within some given limit of accuracy would have the same content as one which predicted all the positions of Venus for the next century within the same limit.

And then, finally, there is the a priori criterion which is the primary concern of this essay, and which I believe to be of immense importance: other things being equal, the simplest hypothesis is the one most probably true. I shall describe what this criterion amounts to more fully and discuss its justification by limiting myself mainly to cases where the hypothesis at stake is a scientific theory consisting of one or more purported laws of nature; and then make the point that it operates in similar fashion to enable us to reach probable conclusions about initial conditions, and about the factors operative in personal explanation.

If one theory is superior to another in yielding the data to a higher degree of inductive probability, or in yielding more data to the same degree of probability, then as such it is more likely to be true, but any greater simplicity of a rival theory is a compensating factor which could lead to equal probability overall or even to the greater probability of the rival. Again, a theory with lower content is as such more likely to be true. But greater ability to yield the data or greater simplicity may come in as compensating factors to make a difference to which is the more probable—except in a case where the theory with greater content entails the theory with lesser. (In this latter case the probability of the latter cannot be less than the former.) A theory of very great content—such as General Relativity, concerned with the behaviour of matter-energy at all points of space and time—may still be judged very probable, despite that great content. And, again, if one theory fits better with background knowledge than does another—one theory about the behaviour of argon at low temperature fits better with our knowledge of what other inert gases do at low temperature than does another—that is reason for supposing it true; but the other factors may come in as compensating factors with the consequence that the theory which fits less well with background knowledge is the one more probably true. (I should add however that the less certain is the background "knowledge," the less the criterion of fit with background knowledge has weight.)

Having made these points about the other principles at work in assessing the probability of scientific theories, I emphasise that I have no theory to put forward about how the factors involved in them are to be measured, nor about how in comparison between two theories better satisfaction of one criterion is to be weighed against worse satisfaction of another. Rather, I aim to show the nature and force of the criterion of simplicity by considering cases of conflicting theories where the other criteria for choice between them are equally well satisfied. I shall then go on to show that the criterion of background knowledge can be reduced to the two criteria of yielding the data and of simplicity. And so in the end, among theories of given content, the choice boils down to weighing yielding the data against simplicity. But since there will always be an infinite number of theories which yield the same data with the same degree of inductive probability—but which make different predictions and retrodictions (and any prediction and retrodiction can be explained by some such theory), without the criterion of simplicity we can make no step beyond the observable data. Without this all-important a priori criterion, we would be utterly lost.

Let me begin by showing the principle of simplicity at work in a trivial example. Let us suppose that we are investigating a new area and there is no background scientific knowledge to guide us as to the form of theory to be expected to hold in this area. We study the relation of two variables—x and y. We collect a finite number of observations of values of y for integral values of x. We find the following results:

x	0	1	2	3	4	5	6
y	0	2	4	6	8	10	12

A formula suggests itself as to how x and y are connected which will allow us to extrapolate to the future: y=2x. The formula yields the data in the respect that from it and from any observed value of x we can deduce the observed value of y. Consequently it satisfies the criterion of yielding these data maximally well. But y=2x is not the only formula which does so. All formulae of the form

$$y=2x +x(x-1)(x-2)(x-3)(x-4)(x-5)(x-6)z$$

yield those data equally well, and there are an infinite number of formulae of that form, according to the filling you give to z, which may be a constant or some function of x. All these different formulae, although agreeing in yielding the values of y (for given values of x) observed so far, make totally different predictions for the future. Why prefer one rather than another? The obvious answer is that we prefer the simplest (y=2x). We believe it to be more likely to be true than those of any other formula of the stated form—as can be seen by the fact that we believe its predictions to be more likely to be true than any other formula of that form. If our life depended on predicting the correct value of y for x=9, we would think it utterly irrational to make any prediction other than y=18.

The comment is often made in discussions of this sort of example that none of the 'wild' theories, for example ones generated by giving non-zero values to z, would be seriously put forward by scientists. The comment is of course true. But my concern is with why the wild theories would not be seriously put forward, and my answer is that scientists implicitly use a principle of simplicity.

People used to say that the answer to this problem was that we should assume that the future will resemble the past. But the future always resembles the past—in some respect. Wherever the next value of y is observed for a given value of x, there will be some mathematical formula which yields that value as well as values of y observed so far. Suppose that when, given the initial data of our previous example, we go on to measure the value of y for $x=7$ and find that $y=5054$. Then the future will have resembled the past in that the past and the future values of y all conform to the formula $y=2x+x(x-1)(x-2)(x-3)(x-4)(x-5)(x-6)$. The criterion "Choose the theory which postulates that the future resembles the past" is empty. To give it content we must amend it to "Choose the theory which postulates that the future resembles the past in the simplest respect." But then we come to realise that the criterion of simplicity is also at work when we retrodict as well as when we predict. It is also at work when we postulate the underlying causes of observable data; and among the infinite number of theories which will do this (in such a way as to yield the data), it tells us (roughly) to postulate few entities and few kinds of entities behaving in mathematically simple kinds of way. If you have a theory which leads you to expect the existence of many thousands of chemical substances in terms of a hundred kinds of atom combining and recombining in various regular patterns, prefer that theory to a theory which also leads you to expect the data but which tells you that each substance is made of varying numbers of atoms of kinds never found in any other substances, which have annihilated each other in complicated ways to produce new atoms forming new substances so far, but are not guaranteed to do so in future.

Some people, faced initially with this issue, suggest that we might test between alternative theories by making a new observation, for example,—to return to the earlier example—find the value of y for $x=7$. If it is 14, then the theory $y=2x$ is confirmed. However, although by making the new observation an infinite number of theories will be shown false, an infinite number will remain, agreeing in yielding all observations so far (including the new one, $y=14$), yet predicting differently for the new future. All theories of the form of the previous theory where z is such that $(x-7)$ is a factor of it are like this. However many theories you eliminate by finding falsifying observations, you will always be left with an infinite number of theories which yield the observations made up to that time, and of those, I claim, we prefer and are right to prefer the simplest as the most probable.

Note that, as I mentioned earlier, our preference for the simplest hypothesis—other things being equal—remains, even if our background knowledge suggests that any correlation between the values of x and y is due to some common cause. We would still make predictions on the basis of y=2x. But once we discover the lawlike regularity connecting these values with a common cause, we may need to amend (in the light of the additional evidence which supports hypotheses about the nature of these lawlike regularities and so of any derivative acausal regularities).

In claiming that the simplest theory which yields the data is that most probably true, I do not, as I have made clear, rule out that theory's being shown false by subsequent observations. If that happens, we need to move to the simplest remaining theory which yields the observations. This process can move science in the direction of a theory quite complicated relative to the theory with which we began, but it is its being simpler than other theories which yield the data available at the time which makes it at that time more probably true than any other theory.

IV. The Nature of Simplicity

Before we can assess the principle of simplicity properly, we must clarify more precisely what it is for the one theory to be simpler than another. Before giving my positive account, I need to rule out a quite different understanding of simplicity which often gets confused with simplicity in my sense, and which clouds the discussion and makes the principle stated implausible. This is the understanding of a theory's being simpler as its having more content. It was Popper, more than anyone, who championed an understanding of this kind. He wrote: "The epistemological questions which arise in connection with the concept of simplicity can all be answered if we equate this concept with degree of falsifiability."[6] He claimed that straight lines were simpler than circles, circles than parabolas or ellipses and so on, because while three observations would suffice to falsify a claim that the equation correlating two variables was a straight line, four would be needed to falsify a claim that the equation was a circle, and five the claim that it was a parabola or ellipse. Likewise the more wide-ranging theory "all swans are white" as opposed to "all swans except Australasian swans are white" was, he claimed, simpler in his sense of more falsifiable.

Popper seemed to equate degree of falsifiability with greater content (or truth in fewer possible worlds).[7] Although these concepts do largely coincide, they are not quite the same. Certainly "all swans are white" is both easier to falsify and has more content than "all swans except Australasian swans are white." But "all swans are white" and "all swans except Australasian swans are white, and Australasian swans are black" seem to have equal content; they both tell us about the colour of all swans, actual and possible. But the former is easier to falsify in the sense that you need to make fewer observations to falsify it. Observing that a bird was a swan, and that its colour was other than white would suffice to falsify that hypothesis; whereas to falsify the latter hypothesis you need to observe not merely what the colour of a swan is, but whether or not it is an Australasian swan.

Elliott Sober's understanding (in *Simplicity*[8]) selects much the same theories as simpler than other theories, as does Popper's understanding. For Sober, the simplest theory is the most informative theory in the sense of the one with respect to which you need to obtain less additional information in order to be able to answer your questions. Thus "all swans are white" is a simpler theory than "all swans are white, except Australasian swans which are black," because the extra information "this is a swan" would enable the first theory to answer the question "what colour is it?"; whereas we need as well the information of where the swan lives before the second theory is able to answer that question. Sober claims that his account of simplicity allows us to discriminate between equally precise equations, such as $y=3x+6$, and $y=5x^4+4x^2+75x+168$. While both theories need to have added to them merely the value of x in order to answer the question "what is the value of y?" they do not require the same amount of extra information in order to answer the question "What is the value of dy/dx?" The first theory needs no extra information to tell you this, whereas the second theory needs to have added to it the value of y (or x).

Now there may be a lot to be said for having simpler theories in any or all of these connected senses. Big claims are theoretically more important than small ones, and if they can be falsified easily, at any rate some progress can often be made. And, of course, we want theories which answer the questions in which we are interested. Note incidentally that Sober's account makes simplicity question-relative (what is simple in a community depends on what its scientific interests are). Our second equation of the last paragraph enables us to answer, without requiring extra information, "What is the value of $y-5x^4-4x^2-75x$?" The answer is 168. But the first equation requires us to have the value of y (or x) before we can answer that question. "All emeralds are green" enables us to answer the question "Is this emerald green?" but not the question "Is this emerald grue?" without further information.

Theories with large content are, however, as such, as I have already noted and as Popper boldly proclaimed, more likely to be false than theories with small content. Hence, as such, it is less rational to rely on the predictions of a theory with large content than on those of a narrower theory. And there is no point in taking the trouble to falsify theories which are almost certainly false anyway. And answers to the questions which interest you are not of much use if they are probably false. It is here that simplicity in a different sense comes in as a criterion of probable truth—among theories of equal content fitting equally well with background knowledge and yielding the data equally well. In my terminology a theory that a planet moves in a circle, for example, does not as such have greater simplicity than the theory that it moves in an ellipse; it just has fewer free parameters (a circle being an ellipse with an eccentricity of zero), and thus has greater content. The theory that it moves in a circle, however, may well be simpler than the theory that it moves in an ellipse of a certain non-circular shape (where both have the same number of free parameters).

What is it for a theory to be simpler in my preferred sense? The same theory in the sense of one that postulates the same entities, properties, and relations between them, may be expressed in different logically equivalent formulations—a formulation of a theory being any collection of sentences which claim that things are (in contingent respects) as the theory claims. One theory is simpler than another if and only if the simplest formulation of the former is simpler than the simplest formulation of the latter. There are various facets of simplicity. They are, to speak strictly, facets of formulations of theories. But in the case of a facet where any formulation of a theory will have the same degree of that facet as any other formulation of the same theory, I shall speak straightforwardly of the simplicity of theories. (The first two facets will be seen to have this property—for example, any formulation of a theory will postulate the same number of entities as any other.)

The first facet of simplicity is just a matter of number of things postulated. A theory which postulates one entity (or property of an entity) rather than two, two rather than three, is (other things being equal) simpler. It is simpler to postulate one unobserved planet acting in accord with Newton's laws rather than two unobserved planets. The principle of simplicity says that if the former yields the data just as well as the latter does, it is more probably true. (The application of this facet in choosing theories is simply the use of Ockham's razor.)

Second, number of kinds of thing. A theory which postulates three kinds of entities (or properties of entities) is (other things being equal) simpler than one which postulates six, and so on. A theory which postulates three kinds of quark is simpler than one which postulates six kinds of quark, and one which postulates that quarks have just certain properties, such as spin, is simpler than one which postulates that they have these properties and also charm as well.[9]

Third, a formulation of a theory which contains a term referring to an entity or descriptive of a property which can only be grasped by someone who grasps some other term will be less simple than an otherwise equally simple formulation of a theory which contains the latter term instead. Thus if "grue" can only be understood by someone who understands "green" but not conversely, then "all emeralds are green" is simpler than "all emeralds are grue."[10] The general force of this requirement is of course, other things being equal, to lead us to prefer predicates designating the more readily observable properties rather than ones a long way distant from observation. We cannot grasp the sense of "enthalpy" or "charm" or "bottomness" unless we understand some of the consequences of a system having a certain amount of enthalpy, or a quark having charm or bottomness in terms closer to observation, or unless there are analogies to these properties among more observable properties; but not vice versa.

Of course which properties are observable depends on who is doing the observing and what apparatus they have to help them. But for any given language-using community in which words are given a sense, that sense may be tied to one means of observing it or to a process which involves all of a number of means of observing, including the former means. Whether or not a track crosses a photographic plate depends on the way it looks to most observers, but whether or not a fundamental particle has a negative charge or not depends (in part) on the results of very many diverse kinds of observation including whether it leaves a track on a photographic plate in certain circumstances. In that sense tracks on photographic plates are more readily observable than the changes of fundamental particles. The less readily observable is more theoretical—the attribution of greenness to an object carries fewer consequences by way of big theory than does the attribution of charm. This facet of simplicity says: do not postulate underlying theoretical properties, unless you cannot get a theory which yields the data equally well without them.

Fourth, a formulation of theory consisting of a few separate laws is (other things being equal) simpler than one consisting of many laws. Kepler's three laws of planetary motion (plus a proposition for each planet, stating its mean distance from the Sun) enabling deduction of the paths and periods of all the planets relative to Earth was (in this respect) simpler than Copernicus's or Ptolemy's forty or so laws which also enabled these to be deduced.

Fifth, a formulation of a theory is simpler in which individual laws relate few variables rather than many. Consider a formulation of a theory T_1 which has three laws, one relating two variables (x and y), one relating two other variables (w and z), and one relating two further variables (r and v). Compare it with a formulation T_2 which also has three laws, each of which relates all six variables. T_1 is, in respect of this facet, the simpler formulation.

And finally (other things being equal) a mathematically simpler formulation is simpler. This facet is illustrated by my earlier example of y=2x being simpler than any formula of the form y=2x+x(x-1)(x-2)(x-3)(x-4)(x-5)(x-6)z, for all fillings of z other than 0.

Two sub-facets are involved in this facet of mathematical simplicity. One is that fewer terms in an equation make it simpler. y=z+x is simpler than y=z+x+x². Secondly, other things being equal, an equation is mathematically simpler than another in so far as it uses simpler mathematical entities or relations than that other. A mathematical entity or relation θ is simpler than another one Ψ if θ can be understood by someone who does not understand Ψ, but Ψ cannot be understood by anyone who does not understand θ. Thus 0 and 1 are simpler entities than 2, 2 than 3 and so on. For you cannot grasp the notion of 2 As unless you can grasp the notion of 0 As. (You would not know what it is for something to be an A in the room unless you knew what it was for there to be 0 As in the room). Conversely, 0 must be understood together with 1, but 1 can be understood without 2 being understood. For this reason $y=z+x$ is a simpler equation than $y=z+2x$. My definition has the consequence that multiplication is a less simple relation than addition, power than multiplication, vector product than scalar product; rational numbers are less simple entities than integers, real numbers than rational numbers, tensors than vectors, etc. Hence $y=x$ is a simpler equation than $y = \sqrt{5x}$. (Note that this criterion of mathematical simplicity concerns the preferable form of an equation relating quantitative values of certain given non-mathematical entities and properties, and is different from the earlier criterion which concerned the preferability of a theory postulating fewer non-mathematical entities and properties).

Interestingly the concept of some quantity being infinitely large is often graspable by someone who has not grasped any concept of a very large number.

For the infinitely long is simply that which is longer than any integral number of standard units of distance, for example, metres, to travelling along which, one metre after another, there are zero bounds. And the infinitely lasting is that which is longer than any integral number of standard units of time, for example, hours, to living through which, one hour after another, there are zero bounds. And the infinitely fast is that whose velocity is greater than any integral number of standard units of distance per unit of time, for example, metres per hour. One does not need to know what a trillion is in order to understand what is the infinitely long or lasting or fast. It is because infinity is simple in this way that scientists postulate infinite degrees of quantities rather than very large degrees of quantities, when both are equally compatible with data.[11] The medievals postulated an infinite velocity of light, and Newton postulated an infinite velocity for the gravitational force, when in each case large finite velocities would have been equally compatible with the data then available measured to the degree of accuracy then obtainable.

In order to compare theories, we need to compare their simplest formulations. But it is not always clear which is the simplest formulation of a theory. For it is always possible to give a formulation of a theory which makes it simpler in one respect at the cost of loss of simplicity in another respect. We can for example reduce many laws to few by introducing variables with more components (scalars such as mass having only one component, vectors such as velocity in three-dimensional space having three components, tensors having many more), and so compressing the information into a shorter form. Maxwell is known for having propounded four laws of electromagnetism, but Maxwell used only vectors and scalars. Put his theory in tensor form, and you can express it with only two laws. But the gain in simplicity in fewness of laws is balanced by the loss involved in introducing variables, that is, values of properties, more remote from observation (you cannot grasp the concept of an electromagnetic field tensor without grasping the concepts of electric field and magnetic field, but not vice versa), and more complex mathematical entities. Formulations of theories may or may not become simpler when there is a loss in respect of one facet but a gain in respect of another.

Even if it is clear that you have theories in their simplest formulations, all too often a new theory whose simplest formulation is simpler than the simplest formulation of its predecessor in respect of one facet will be more complex in respect of another. Take again that well-worn example of Copernicus's theory of planetary motion (with its many epicycles, deferents, and moving eccentrics, carrying the planets round the sun) versus Kepler's theory of noncircular elliptical motion of planets around the sun. In (what are fairly evidently) their simplest formulations Copernicus's has laws covering some forty separate circular motions, whereas Kepler's theory has far fewer laws. But non-circular elliptical motion is more complex than circular motion—there are more terms in an equation of non-circular elliptical motion. How can we weigh the facets against each other? With the benefit of hindsight, I am inclined to say that Kepler's theory is simpler than Copernicus's; the gain in having so few separate motions is not outweighed by the small addition to the complexity of individual motions. But that was not obvious in the seventeenth century.

It is, I suggest, normally objectively clear which is the simplest formulation of a theory and which theory is the simplest, when simplest formulations differ only in respect of one facet of simplicity. And, although the criteria for comparing facets of simplicity are in no way clear, there is, I suggest plenty of consensus over a range of cases about how to weigh greater simplicity in one respect against less in another, although I do not think that any general formula can be produced for calculating this which would command any widespread agreement. My ground for supposing that there is this general consensus is this. Take some standard scientific theory T_1; produce another theory T_2 which yields the data equally well and has equal content, and has some marginal advantage over T_1 in respect of one facet of simplicity at the expense of disadvantage in respect of another. It will normally be evident to any scientist (even if he knows nothing about the particular field in question) which is the simpler theory and the one to be adopted if they fit equally well with background knowledge. But there certainly remains a borderland of pairs of formulations of theories about the relative overall simplicity of which scientists will differ.[12]

Bearing in mind that the relative simplicity of theories is a matter of the relative simplicity of their simplest formulations, I shall now revert to comparison of theories rather than of their formulations. My suggestion is, in the light of the preceding analysis, that in the vast majority of cases there is sufficient agreement about when one theory which yields the data (and has equal content and fits background knowledge equally well) is simpler than another which does so equally well. It follows that, although it will often be the case that, compatible with our data, there are three or four theories which scientists will agree to be overall equally simple or about the relative simplicity of which they will differ, innumerable theories will be evidently less simple than these and so—at this stage—less probable than the serious competitors. Crucial experiments can then be done to accumulate new data which will render all except one of these theories improbable. But without the principle of simplicity there would always be innumerable theories with claims to equal probability on the data.

Although the account of simplicity which I have just given is fairly brief and fairly vague, it is, I think considerably fuller and more plausible than the only other well-known philosophical account of simplicity of the kind with which I have been concerned, that is, as a guide to truth—that of Harold Jeffreys. He supposed that any equation of interest "can be expressed as a differential equation of finite order and degree, in which the numerical coefficients are integers."[13] He argues that equations of other types in physics are hardly ever derived directly from observations and arise only at a theoretical level. Jeffreys's method for ranking equations of the former type has been stated somewhat differently in different publications, and interpretations of what Jeffreys really meant vary. But here is one reasonable interpretation by Mary Hesse of what Jeffreys "essentially" proposed: "The complexity of a law should be defined as the sum of the absolute values of the integers (degrees and derivative orders) contained in it, together with the number of its freely adjustable parameters. Thus $y^2 = ax^3$ would have complexity value 6; $d^2y/dx^2 + 2.345y = 0$, complexity 4, and so on."[14] We may suppose—though Hesse does not say so—that laws are to be compared in respect of their simplest formulations, and that the simplest formulation is the one with the lowest complexity ranking.

Jeffreys's ranking does yield some counter-intuitive results. Thus '$y = x^{13}$' (complexity value 14) is on his ranking more complex than '$d^2y/dx^2 = ax + b\,x^2 + cx^3 + 3$' (complexity value 12). More substantially, it simply does not deal with important types of equation. Whether or not equations other than differential equations have in the past been formulated on the basis of observations, clearly some transcendental equations (for example, $y=e^x$) are simpler than some differential equations, and hence if theories were proposed with equations of the two types, there could be cases where the theory with the transcendental equation was intrinsically the more probable. And Jeffreys provides no guide as to how to rank full-scale theories with different numbers of laws postulating different numbers of entities. And, finally, there is the problem for many but not all of us that Jeffreys's ranking prevents our analysing the probability of scientific theories on evidence in terms of the probability calculus. For the prior probability of a hypothesis on tautological evidence (that is, no relevant empirical evidence), which we may call its intrinsic probability, will, on the general account I have given, be determined by the two a priori criteria—content and simplicity—and so among theories of equal content (such as theories stating a mathematical relation between the same two variables) by simplicity. Yet (given standard analysis) there is no way of ascribing prior probabilities on the basis of Jeffreys's ranking to many sets of such theories in such a way that these conform to the axioms of the probability calculus. For on Jeffreys's ranking every integral multiple of a variable scores equally. Hence $y=x$ has the same complexity score (2) as $y=2x$, $y=3x$, and so on; and so these being theories of equal content, they should have equal prior probability. Yet any attribution of the same prior probability to each member of this infinite sequence of theories has the consequence that their disjunction has an infinite probability.[15] My account avoids this difficulty by attributing different degrees of simplicity and so different prior probabilities to different integral multiples. (y=4x is less simple than y=3x, and so on).

David Lewis has claimed that simple theories should have predicates which designate "natural" properties:

> We should ask how candidate systems compare in simplicity when each is formulated in the simplest eligible way; or, if we count different formulations as different systems, we should dismiss the ineligible ones from candidacy. An appropriate standard of eligibility is not far to seek: let the primitive vocabulary that appears in the axioms refer to perfectly natural properties.[16]

And of course the problem then arises as to how we are to recognise these "perfectly natural properties." My answer is that only comparative talk is in place—one can recognise properties postulated by one theory as more natural than those postulated by another. They are either the more readily observable properties (ones which are designated by predicates which an investigator can grasp, while needing to grasp the sense of fewer other predicates) or properties which have worked better in other theories.[17] The former are natural because they contain intrinsically simpler properties; the latter derive their naturalness from theories which incorporate them

fitting well with successful background theories—
it is background knowledge which determines their
naturalness. So far I have been concerned to hold
background knowledge constant (for example, because there is no background knowledge relevant to
the field of inquiry or because theories up for con-
sideration fit it equally well). If we ignore background knowledge, naturalness is a matter of ready
observability.

So then, I have claimed,—if we set aside background knowledge—among theories with equal
content which yield the data equally well, that theory
which is simplest by my criteria is that most probably true. New data may always be discovered, in
consequence of which a different theory proves to
be "the simplest theory which yields those data."
Disagreements at an initial stage about simplicity
may prove irrelevant when new data turn up. But
the fact remains that at any given stage, if in any
respect at all we need to rely on theories, we must
make a judgement about which way of extrapolating from the data so far obtained leads to the theory
more likely to be true. My claim is that I have captured the criteria involved in the judgements of almost all of us; we regard predictions made in accor-
dance with them as more probably true than any
other we could make, and we regard someone who
follows quite different criteria as totally irrational.
There are plenty of criteria, following which will
lead us to predict that gravity will not operate on
Sundays in Scotland or after the galaxies are further

apart than they are now, or any other crazy prediction. But rationality of prediction involves being
guided by simplicity in my umbrella sense.

V. The Role of Background Knowledge

I have written of simplicity as a criterion of choice
when there is no background knowledge. But, it may
be urged, that is not our normal situation. In prac-
tise, it is said, scientists already know (from their
previous knowledge of the field of enquiry) the kind
of theory for which they are looking. If they are
studying the viscosity of some gas at low temperature, they know from the formulae governing other
gases the kind of shape such a curve ought to have.
When they have acquired enough data for the new
gas, the equation of its curve may even then be
uniquely determined by the data. Or again, in at-
tempting to find the cause of some genetic abnor-
mality, we know the sort of thing we are looking
for—genes (in the form of DNA chains) at loca-
tions on chromosomes. We know this as a result of
the establishment of a genetic theory which works
so well in explaining so many other phenomenal
characteristics in these terms. Our theory of this ab-
normality needs therefore to fit this theory which
explains other phenomenal characteristics. Given
that we explain in these terms, then with enough
new experimental data, the location and structure
of the genes may well be uniquely determined. Or
even if there is no unique determination, the sug-

gestion goes, such background knowledge is by far the major determinant of choice among theories equally able to yield the data.

Against this, there are two points to be made. The first is that when we are considering very large-scale theories, there will be no such background knowledge. A general theory of the mechanical behaviour of matter, such as was Newton's, attempted to explain so much that there were no theories of neighbouring areas with which it could dovetail. Since then, there were developed theories of light and then theories of electro-magnetism, and Einstein sought a theory which explained all that these lower-level theories of matter and electro-magnetism sought to explain. But again the vastness of the area which his theory sought to cover left no neighbouring areas with probable theories with which his theory could dovetail. Theories have been developed for yet new areas since that time. We have now theories of the weak nuclear force and of the strong nuclear force, as well as Quantum Theory. And a Theory of Everything, like superstring theory, seeks to explain all things now known to science. And again there are no theories of neighbouring areas with which such a theory could dovetail. Yet an infinite number of such very large-scale theories could be constructed which yield the data obtained so far. How can we choose between them except on grounds of simplicity?

Since I have illustrated my thesis so far mainly with very trivial examples, it might be worthwhile now to illustrate it in more detail with one of the slightly less trivial examples which I have just cited. Consider Newton formulating his theory of gravitation to account for the data of terrestrial gravitation (incorporated in Galileo's law of fall), of collision (formulated by Huyghens), of planetary motion (captured by Kepler's laws), of the motions of Jupiter and Saturn, of tides and comets. His three laws of motion and his law of gravitational attraction (that all bodies attract each other with forces proportional to the product of their masses (m and m') and inversely proportional to the square of their distance apart (r)—$F=mm'/r^2$—were such as to allow us from innumerable observed values of variables to deduce others which we could observe to hold (to the limit of accuracy which could be measured); they yielded a vast number of data very well. But equally successful and of equal content would have been any theory which replaced the law of gravitational attraction with a law of the form $F=mm'/r^2+Kmm'/r4$ where K is a very small constant, such that the data available to Newton would not have been sufficiently accurate to allow discrimination between the predictions of the two theories. Indeed sixty years later, when data had been obtained which did seem sufficiently accurate to discriminate between Newton's theory and a certain theory of the latter form, they seemed to Clairaut to be such as to favour the latter, and he tentatively proposed such a theory—but only because of the (as it seemed to him) inability of Newton's theory to yield the data

then available[18]; otherwise his preference for
Newton's theory was clear. Among other theories
which yield the data available in the eighteenth century (to as great a degree of accuracy as could then
or can now be measured) are all theories obtained
from Newton's theory by replacing the law of gravi-
tation by a law of the form $F=mm'/r^{2.000...(100\text{ zeros})...1}$.
So too do many theories in which $F=mm'/r^2+Km$
where K is a variable whose value depends on the
average distance apart of the galaxies. As, in consequence of their mutual recession arising from the
"Big Bang," the galaxies get further apart, they may
eventually reach some critical level (for example, in
2000 A.D.). K, we may suppose, has the value zero
until then, in 2000 A.D. it has value 1, and thereaf-
ter it has a value which measures the proportional
increase since 2000 A.D. of the average distance apart
of the galaxies. Such theories will be just as good as
Newton's theory at yielding the data obtained so far.
Of course, all these theories are not supported by
the data, but why they are not supported is not because they do not yield the data (in the sense which
I defined), for they do; but because they are obviously less simple than another theory which does
yield the data.

The point which I have made with regard to
Newton's theory and the support given to it by the
data available in the eighteenth century will
obviously also apply to any contemporary theory
which purports to explain so much that there is no
background knowledge of how things work in

neighbouring areas with which the theory can dovetail. A Theory of Everything does not have to answer to any background knowledge. Ability to yield
the data observed up to now (namely, the data
yielded also by lower-level theories) and simplicity
are the only criteria by which it can be compared
with other theories of equal content, namely, other
theories of Everything.

But the second and all-important point is that
where there is background knowledge, where there
are theories of neighbouring fields, it is the criterion
of simplicity which determines which proposed
theory "fits best" with those neighbouring theories.
'Fitting better' is 'fitting more simply,' and thus
making for a simpler overall view of the world.

Suppose you are studying the structure of some
chemical substance x. Chemical theory already tells
you of the element atoms of which all other chemical
substances are built, their valency, and the kinds of
bond which can exist between them. Experimental
evidence may be provided of some of the substances
out of which x was formed and into which it
decomposes. Does not this background knowledge
already fix the parameters in terms of which the
chemical formula of x is to be stated? Perhaps a finite
number of experiments will eliminate all possibilities
except one. Not so. Maybe x has a component atom
never found elsewhere in the Universe, formed out
of its own special kind of quark, which comes into
being when x is formed and disappears when it de-

composes. Maybe there are kinds of bond which bind together the atoms of x and no other substance. And so on. But this sort of supposition is absurd. Of course it is. But why is it absurd? Because the supposition that in one substance there exist kinds of atoms formed in kinds of ways and forming kinds of bonds unknown in the rest of the Universe amounts to a supposition that our general chemical and physical laws are vastly less simple than we had otherwise supposed them to be. They would have the form not "L1...L20" (where these are relatively simple laws applying to all chemical substances) but the form of "L1...L20, except in x where L21...L24," where L21...L24 are laws of a totally different form from L1...L20. It is the criterion of simplicity which tells us to have theories which "mesh" with theories of neighbouring and wider fields, and it does so by insisting that overall theories be as simple as possible. The criterion of background knowledge—that that theory of some field T1 which fits better with theories established for neighbouring fields T', T''... etc., than do other theories of the former field T2, T3, T4 . . . etc., is (other things being equal) more likely to be true than the latter theories, boils down to the criteria of yielding the data and of simplicity. For the claim is that that conjunction of theories (T1 with T', T''... etc., rather than T2 with T', T''... etc.) which is the simplest theory to yield the data in all fields (to a given degree of probability) is (among theories of equal content) that most likely to be true.[19]

In holding simpler theories to be more probable than complex theories, the inquirer is holding it to be more probable that the world as a whole is simple than that it is complex. Hence we should postulate, on grounds of simplicity, as more likely to be true, that theory of a narrow region which makes our overall world theory the simplest for the total data. That theory may not be the simplest theory of the narrow aspect of the world, considered on its own. When it is urged that there are grounds for postulating many entities rather than few, or a complex equation rather than a simple one, even when a simpler theory yields the data equally well, those grounds will, I suggest, be found to consist in the fact that theories of neighbouring fields postulate many entities in similar circumstances or equations of similar form, and so the overall picture is simpler if we postulate in a new region the same kind of complexity as in the others.[20]

Now that I have discussed the role of simplicity in choosing between big theories or conjunctions, this is the place at which to make the obvious point that a scientist can only make a choice between the theories which have occurred to him or to his colleagues (if only to be dismissed as absurd). There may be simple theories of which the scientist has not thought, and his judgement that a certain theory is the one most probably true on the evidence may arise through a failure to realize that there is a much simpler theory which yields the data. Scientific

progress is so often a matter of thinking of new possible theories. For the same reason a scientist may
misjudge which theory fits best with background
knowledge, through a failure to realize the simplicity of some overall connections. In this case his error will affect his judgement of the comparative
worth of theories, not merely his judgement of the
absolute worth of the theories available to him. For
it may be that a theory T1 of a narrow area fits better with background knowledge B than does a theory
T2 of that area—although the scientist has made
the reverse judgement, through a failure to see that
there is a very simple overall theory θ of which (B
and T1) is a consequence. Or—worse—if the background "knowledge" in the form of theories of many
observable phenomena is in error because the simplest theory of those phenomena has not been
thought of, the scientist may prefer as fitting best
with the current background theory a certain theory
of a narrow area, when he would choose a quite different theory if the simplest background theory had
been thought of. Again, his failure to entertain some
theory has led him to make erroneous judgements
not merely of the absolute probability but of the
comparative probability of theories of a narrow
area.[21] Scientists' judgements of probability are much
less likely to be in error through misapplication of
the other criteria of content and yielding the data.

VI. Attempts to Explain Simplicity Away

Among philosophers who allow this—hard to resist—claim that simplicity plays the crucial role which I have described in choosing between theories, there are three kinds of unsatisfactory response. The first is to claim that there are reasons why we choose simple theories other than the greater probable truth of a simple theory. The second is to claim that an a posteriori justification can be given for our use of the criterion of simplicity as a criterion of probable truth. And the third is to claim that an a priori justification can be given by showing that it follows from some theorem of the probability calculus or even more obvious logical truth that the simplest theory is that most probably true. I think that responses of all these kinds are mistaken.

Let us begin with the claim that our preference for simpler theories is for reasons other than their greater probable truth. The obvious version of this is that we prefer simpler theories because it is more convenient to operate with them. It may be more convenient, but it is not always that much more convenient. It would not be too difficult in these days of computer-aided calculations to work out the predictions of some theories more complicated than the simplest theory (of given content which yield the data to a given degree of probability) if it were important to do so. Yet, even given the predictions of quite a large number of different theories worked out in advance for us, we would still think it right to rely on the predictions of the simplest theory. Our main interest in predictions is an interest in probable truth. We need to know whether the bridge will break if we drive a lorry over it, whether the drug will kill or cure, whether the nuclear explosion will set up a chain reaction which will destroy all humanity, and so on. If there are two theories which yield the observations made so far, one predicts that all life in the northern hemisphere will be destroyed tomorrow and the other predicts that all life in the southern hemisphere will be destroyed tomorrow, and there is no time to test further between them but the latter is complicated and the former is simple, any northerner would be on the aeroplane to the south tonight and think that they were highly rational to do so. They would be on the aeroplane because they believe that the predictions of the former theory are probably true, and that is because they believe the former theory itself is probably true (or at any rate has a greater probability of truth than the latter theory).

But, given that there is no escaping the fact that scientists use simplicity as a criterion of probable truth, the second unsatisfactory philosophical reaction is to claim that there are empirical grounds for their doing so. It is, the argument goes, the fact that in general simpler theories have worked well in the past which justifies us in assuming that they will work well in the future. To put the claim formally—consider any set of data available at some moment of past history t, and any pair of theories which yield those data equally well, T_A and T_B (either actual theories which were constructed or theories which could have been constructed at t), such that T_A is the simplest theory which yields the data and T_B a more complex theory; then normally T_A has or would have subsequently proved the better predictor. We can generalise from these past results to: usually, simplest theories predict better than more complex theories, and this in turn justifies our belief that on some new occasion the simplest theory will predict better. True, sometimes the simplest theory hasn't proved the better predictor. Equally able to yield the rough data known to Boyle about how the temperature (T) of gases varied with their pressure (p) and volume (v) were no doubt both Boyle's law, pv=RT (R being a constant which varies with the gas) and (if it had been formulated then) Van der Waals's law $(p+a/v^2)(v-b)=RT$, a and b again being constants which vary with the kind of gas. Yet Van der Waals's law proved the better subsequent predictor. But the claim was only that usually the simplest theory has proved the better predictor, and that would justify the assertion that probably a given simplest theory will prove the better predictor on some future occasion.

However, even this modest claim about the history of science—that usually the simplest theory has proved the better predictor seems very doubtful. In many areas of inquiry the simpler "laws" which served well in the past have been replaced by more complicated laws—the Boyle to Van der Waals story is hardly unique. But even if simplest theories have usually proved better predictors, this would not provide a justification for subsequent use of the criterion of simplicity, for the reason that the justification itself already relies on the criterion of simplicity. There are different ways of extrapolating from the corpus of past data about the relative success which was had by actual theories and which would have been had by possible theories of different kinds, if they had been formulated. "Usually simplest theories predict better than more complex theories" is one way. Another way is an extrapolation of the form "Usually theories formulated by Greeks in the bath, by Englishmen who watch apples drop, or Germans who work in patent offices... etc., which initially appeal to the scientific community predict better than other theories."[22] An extrapolation of this kind, spelled out at great length, would yield the data of the past history of science just as well as the extrapolation which connects predictive success with simplicity. Of course, this kind of extrapolation is an absurd way of extrapolating from the past data concerning the relative success of theories. And why is it absurd? Because it is far less simple than the obvious way of extrapolating. We have assumed the principle in providing its justification! Any other purported empirical justification of use of the criterion of simplicity will prove equally circular.

Finally, there is the reaction of claiming that it follows from some theorem of the traditional probability calculus or even from some more obvious

logical truth that the simplest theory will probably
predict best, and so is more likely to be true than
other theories. This is a more sophisticated way of
putting the old claim that a deductive justification
can be provided for supposing that induction will
probably work. But the past is just a finite collection of data. How could it be a logical consequence
of it either what will happen or what will probably
happen? As Hume, of course, affirmed: "there can
be no demonstrative arguments to prove, that those
instances of which we have had no experience, resemble those, of which we have had experience,"[23]
and I add, to tighten the argument, "in any given
respect." Yet philosophers still go on trying to produce such arguments. The latest attempt is an in-
teresting one by Malcolm Forster and Elliott Sober[24] who claim that Akaike's Theorem avails for
this purpose. This theorem is concerned with the
problem of fitting a curve to a given collection of
data in such a way as to make predictions of future
data which (very probably) have a high degree of
predictive accuracy. It supposes that we have in mind
some family of low-dimensional curves (for example,
straight lines, which form a 2-dimensional family
in the sense that we need to give values to two variables to select a particular line. The equation of a
straight line being $x=ky + c$, we need to give values
to k and c to select a particular line.) We compare
this family with some family of higher dimensional
curves (for example, parabolas), which may or may
not include the low dimensional family. We choose

the member of the low dimensional family which best fits the data—call it L, and then the member of the higher dimensional family which fits the data exactly as well as L—call it P. It is then shown that, subject to the (implicit) assumption that the two particular curves have equal prior probabilities (or probability densities) and certain other very modest assumptions, L will probably predict better than P.[25] This is an awesome result, when you first look at it. However the awe begins to disappear when you note that it will hold for any lower and any higher dimensional families whatever. So if we choose a low-dimensional family of very contorted curves and compare it with a higher-dimensional family of smooth curves (for example, parabolas), it will prove that the best fitting member of the former family will probably predict better than an equally well fitting member of the latter family.[26] Any particular curve can serve as the sole member of a 0-dimensional family, and Akaike's theorem will show that it will probably predict better than whatever turns out to be the member of some large family which is equally well fitting. Despite the title of Forster and Sober's paper, Akaike's theorem has no tendency whatever to show that simpler theories in my sense are more accurate predictors. Their result follows from the particular method by which the two competing curves are chosen—as members of two previously chosen families of different dimensions—and the result depends on their being chosen by that method. It tells you that if you seek to find the true theory by this method, then the theory from the lower-dimensional family is, on the evidence of how it is chosen, likely to predict better. But it gives no reason to suppose that this is a very sensible way of choosing curves, in any way likely to yield a curve which is a good predictor. It will only do this if we have exercised the prior choice of families of curves in the right way. Intuitively that involves the families being families of curves which fit simply together (which, for example, are all parabolas instead of a mixture of parabolas and sin-curves), and the lower-dimensional family being a family of simple curves. We have to feed an understanding of simplicity into Akaike's theorem in order to get anything worthwhile out of it. And even its very limited result will only hold on the assumption that all particular curves have the same prior probability (or probability density)—which some one who holds that simplicity in my sense is evidence of truth will deny.

All such attempts to prove from some theorem of mathematics or logic that the simpler theory is more probably true are, I suggest, doomed to failure. The fact—however unwelcome to many—is that, if the principle of simplicity is true, it is a fundamental a priori truth. If data ever render one theory or one prediction more probable than another, that can only be because there are a priori criteria for extrapolating from the data in one direction rather than another. Yet there is no truth of logic with a consequence about which direction of extrapolation yields probable truth. So—if any proposition which is not analytic is synthetic—it is both synthetic and a priori that (other things being equal) a simpler theory is more probably true than a complex one. If simplicity could be justified further, it would derive that justification from some higher a priori criterion, and that one would be fundamental. We have to stop somewhere if particular judgements about the probability of theories and their predictions are ever to be justified, and the criterion of simplicity is, I suggest, the right stopping place. This paper has sought to show that this criterion is implicit in our comparisons of pairs of theories for their relative probability. It is more evident that the simplest theory (among theories of equal content which yield the data equally well and fit equally well with background knowledge) is the one most likely to be true than that a theory fitting any other description is the one most likely to be true.

VII. The Ubiquity of the Simplicity Principle

My claim that for given fit with background knowledge among hypotheses of the same content which yield the data equally well, the simplest is that most probably true—has been argued so far only for inanimate explanation and, holding initial conditions constant, only for scientific theories. But the same considerations apply when we hold scientific theories constant, and compare theories of initial conditions; or when both theories and initial conditions are allowed to vary, and we seek the most probable account overall of what are the initial conditions and what is the true theory. Assuming Newton's theory to be true, Leverrier wondered why Uranus moved along a path which was irregular in comparison with the path which Newtonian theory seemed to predict for it. On the supposition that the only other planets were the five known to the ancients together with Uranus, the irregularities were not to be expected. So Leverrier postulated a seventh planet, which pulled Uranus out of its regular orbit when close to it.[27] He could have postulated seven hundred heavenly bodies with a common centre of gravity at the position at which he postulated Neptune, but the former supposition was simpler (in virtue of the first facet which I described). Or he could have put forward a yet more complicated proposal, amending Newton's theory and postulating two further heavenly bodies at the same time. But of course he would not have supposed that the evidence supported that complicated hypothesis. The simplest overall hypothesis (of theory and initial conditions) was that most probably true.

The same considerations apply to personal explanation. In considering hypotheses seeking to explain the occurrence of certain data through the intentional agency of a person, we prefer, among those which yield the data, other things being equal, the simplest. We find certain pieces of metal all having on them the same outline of a human head. A possible explanation is that they were caused intentionally by a person, exercising (by holding a chisel) normal human bodily powers, desiring to make a coin and believing that a piece of metal with such marks would be a coin. There are many other possible explanations which would lead us to expect the phenomena—maybe each of the marks on the pieces of metal were made by different persons at different periods of history with different beliefs to satisfy different desires and that it was in consequence a coincidence that all the marks had the same shape. While detailed hypotheses of this kind can satisfy the criterion of leading us to expect the observed phenomena, as well as does the former hypothesis, clearly they satisfy the criterion of simplicity far less well—for they postulate many persons, desires, and beliefs rather than one person, one desire, and one belief. (Of course in these and all other examples which we consider, 'other things' may not be 'equal.' The criterion of fit with background knowledge may affect crucially the assessment of such hypotheses; knowledge, for example, about how and when and where other persons make coins. So too may the criterion of content. The former hypothesis attributing the marks to the agency of one person with certain desires and beliefs is more probable than a hypothesis which purports to tell us a lot more about who that person was and what were his other desires and beliefs.)

In assessing a much wider range of phenomena in terms of their intentional causation by human persons, we build up a picture of the phenomena as caused by few persons with powers and desires and beliefs which are constant or change in regular ways (that is, vary in a mathematically simple way with variations in the values of few variables, for example, sensory stimuli)—as few persons and as simple ways of change as we can. If we can explain two events brought about by a human in order to fulfil the same desire, we do not invoke a quite new desire to explain the second event. If we can explain an event as brought about by a person in virtue of powers of the same kind as other humans have, we do not postulate some novel power—we do not postulate that some person has a basic power of bending spoons at some distance away if we can explain the phenomenon of the spoons' being bent by someone else bending them with his hands. And so on.

And if the issue is whether certain phenomena are brought about intentionally by a person at all rather than being caused by some inanimate process, the issue turns on whether there is a simple personal explanation which leads us to expect these phenomena. If we go to a distant planet and find some object with appendages moving around and causing effects, the question arises whether we have here a person (or animal) or just an inanimate object. The issue then turns on whether we can attribute to this object a small set of constant desires and beliefs sensitive to sense data about how to fulfil them, with a set of powers to act intentionally guided by beliefs and desires, in such a way as to lead us to expect the phenomena which we observe.

VIII. Bayes's Theorem

Our use of the criterion of simplicity can be well articulated by Bayes's theorem. This holds that the posterior probability of a hypothesis h, on background knowledge k and evidence of observation e is

$$P\ (h\ /e\ \&\ k) = \frac{P\ (e\ /h\ \&\ k)}{P\ (e\ /k)} \times P\ (h\ /k)$$

$P(e/k)$ is a factor common to the determination of the posterior probability of all hypotheses on evidence e, and so may be ignored for purposes of comparison between such hypotheses. $P(e/h\&k)$ is a measure of how well the hypothesis yields the data. $P(h/k)$ is a measure of how probable is h, given background knowledge alone. If k contains empirical background knowledge, then $P(h/k)$ will depend in part on how well h fits with k, which—as we have seen—is a matter of how simple is the conjunction (h&k). But if we put all the empirical data into e, then k becomes some bare tautology. In that case $P(h/k)$ is what we may call the intrinsic probability of h; it will depend solely on factors intrinsic to h. That there is this crucial a priori element affecting the probability of h is the claim of this paper, which affirms that it is a function of simplicity and (inversely) of content.

Nobody supposes that in general (that is, apart from certain special cases, such as where the probability is 1 or 0 or 0.5), it is possible to allocate exact numerical values to the probability of a theory on evidence. But the claim that Bayes's theorem articulates the criteria which we use for judging theories probable amounts to the following: in so far as exact numerical values can be allocated, it gives the right answers and yields only those theorems of comparative probability which we judge to be correct—for example, it yields 'If $P(h_1/k)=P(h_2/k)$ then $P(h_1/e\&k)>P(h_2/e\&k)$ if and only if $P(e/h_1\&k)>P(e/h_2\&k)$—given $P(e/k)\neq0$.' Put another way—arbitrary values can always be allocated to the probabilities involved, values which make those values more precise than do our normal inductive criteria (though not inconsistent with them), in such way as to conform to Bayes's theorem. The claim that intrinsic probability is in part a function of simplicity then amounts to the claim that (for given content) greater simplicity means greater prior probability, and so—for given e and non-empirical k—greater posterior probability. Bayes's theorem allows us to give formal articulation to this claim.

To summarise the claims in a nutshell: either science is irrational (in the way it judges theories and predictions probable) or the principle of simplicity is a fundamental synthetic a priori truth.

Notes

1. For justification of the distinction between these two patterns see, for example, Richard Taylor, *Action and Purpose*, (Englewood Cliffs, N.J.: Prentice Hall, 1966), ch. 14; or my *The Existence of God* (Oxford: Clarendon Press, second edition, 1990) ch.2.

2. C. G. Hempel, "Aspects of Scientific Explanation" in his *Aspects of Scientific Explanation* (New York: The Free Press, 1965) distinguished deductive-nomological (D-N) explanation, from inductive-statistical (I-S) explanation in which laws and initial conditions make the explanandum event probable while not entailing its occurrence. Wesley Salmon rightly pointed out that the crucial thing was not that the former make the latter probable, but that they make it more probable than it would otherwise be. Explanation of this kind he called statistical-relevance (S-R) explanation. (See his *Statistical Explanation and Statistical Relevance*, Pittsburgh: University of Pittsburgh Press, 1971).

3. This account was brought back into modern discussion in R. Harré and E. H. Madden, *Causal Powers* (Oxford: Basil Blackwell, 1975). For my own reasons for preferring a SPL account to an LIC one, see my "The Irreducibility of Causation," *Dialectica*, forthcoming.

4. Desires are inbuilt inclinations to act in certain ways with which at any given time an agent finds himself.

An agent will act on his strongest desire, unless he
believes it good not to do so, and then he has to choose
on which desire to act. For articulation of this model
of personal explanation, see my *The Evolution of the
Soul* (Oxford: Clarendon Press, 1986), chs. 5 and 6.

5. I am concerned in this section to propound the thesis
that an explanation of some event makes possible the
prediction of *further* events and indeed provides the
paradigmatic means of making predictions. My concern arises because I wish to point out that the same
criteria, notably simplicity, are at work in judging the
worth of purported explanations as of purported predictions. The question usually considered under the
heading of "symmetry of explanation and prediction"
is whether the same factors which enable one to
explain a given event would—if known in advance—
have enabled one to predict it (and vice versa). Though
the question is slightly different from that to which my
thesis gives an answer, the same kind of examples and
counter-examples prove relevant.

6. K. R. Popper, *The Logic of Scientific Discovery* (London: Hutchinson, 1959), p. 140.

7. Op. cit., p. 113.

8. Elliott Sober, *Simplicity* (Oxford: Clarendon Press,
1975).

9. A theory with few variables often has an advantage
over a theory with many variables of a kind to which
Glymour drew our attention. This is that the value of

a variable of the former can be calculated from different parts of the data by different routes. Plausibly, if the two ways of calculating it yield the same value, that confirms the theory. See Clark Glymour, *Theory and Evidence* (Princeton, N.J.: Princeton University Press, 1980), passim. But this is an advantage possessed by families of theories (that is, "theories" in which values of variables are yet to be determined) over other families. It is not an advantage possessed by one fully determinate theory postulating many properties with precise values over one postulating few properties with precise values, which is what the first and second facets of simplicity described in the text are concerned with. To the extent to which a theory (that is, a family of theories) T_1 possesses Glymour's advantage over another theory T_2, then T_1 rules out more combinations of observations than does T_2. For if there are two kinds of observation each of which allows us to calculate the value of a certain variable of T_1, then for each value of one kind of observation, all values except one of the other kind of observation are ruled out. If this does not hold for T_2, T_2 rules out less than does T_1. So T_1 predicts more precisely than does T_2. Glymour's advantage thus comes under the heading of yielding the data rather than of simplicity in my sense. Glymour himself acknowledges that his "bootstrap procedures ...do not seem to help the [curve fitting] problem much more than a whit" (op. cit., p. 340).

10. See the famous example introduced into philosophical discussion by Nelson Goodman in his *Fact, Fiction, and Forecast* (Indianapolis: Bobbs-Merrill, second edition, 1965). The original example has usually

been altered slightly in subsequent discussion, so that
an object is defined as "grue" at a time t if and only if
it is green and t is before 2000 A.D. or it is blue and t
is after 2000 A.D. Hence all emeralds observed so far
(that is, before 1997) are green, and also now grue. But
it seems a better justified extrapolation from those
data to "all emeralds are (always) green" than to "all
emeralds are (always) grue." The former hypothesis
would have the consequence that emeralds after 2000
A.D. would be green; the latter hypothesis would have
the consequence that emeralds after 2000 A.D. would
be blue. Our conception of grue is a more complicated
conception than that of green since in order to grasp
what it is to be grue, we have first to grasp what it is to
be green, but not vice versa. Hence our preference for
the former hypothesis can be explained in terms of our
preference for the simpler hypothesis. We do not need
to invoke the "entrenchment" of "green" to explain
our preference for it. If "grue" is introduced not by
definition but by example, then the examples by
which (before 2000 A.D.) it is introduced will be the
same as those by which "green" is introduced, and no-
one will have any reason for supposing that it has a
different meaning from "green" and so that there is
any conflict between hypotheses which use the one
term and hypotheses which use the other. After 2000
A.D. there will of course be grounds for preferring one
of the two hypotheses over the other in virtue of its
fitting the data better.

11. Of course to distinguish between different cardinal
    and ordinal infinite numbers, and to grasp transfinite
    arithmetic does require certain sophisticated con-

cepts, but one can grasp the concept of a quantity being infinitely large without grasping all that.

12. T. S. Kuhn, in *The Essential Tension* (Chicago: University of Chicago Press, 1977), p. 322, listed simplicity among five "standard criteria for assessing the adequacy of a scientific theory," along with accuracy, consistency, scope and fruitfulness, and he commented that individually the criteria are imprecise and they often conflict with each other.

13. Harold Jeffreys, *Scientific Inference* (Cambridge: Cambridge University Press, 1931), p. 45.

14. See her article on "Simplicity" in (ed.) Paul Edwards, *Encyclopedia of Philosophy* (London: MacMillan, 1967).

15. For this and other deficiencies in Jeffreys's system, see Colin Howson, "On the Consistency of Jeffreys's Simplicity Postulate and its Role in Bayesian Inference," *Philosophical Quarterly* 38 (1988), pp. 68-83.

16. David Lewis, "New Work for a Theory of Universals," *Australasian Journal of Philosophy* 61 (1983), pp. 343-77. See p. 367.

17. Bas Van Fraassen, in *Laws and Symmetry* (Oxford: Clarendon Press, 1989), p. 53, writes: "The suspicion I have at this point is this: if there really is an objective distinction between natural classes and others, and if laws in the sense of Lewis are what science hopes to formulate in the long run, then the only possible evidence for a predicate being natural is that it appears

in a successful theory." Van Fraassen is right to suspect the empirical basis of much naturalness, but wrong to suggest that all naturalness is thus based. For given any successful background theory, there can be an infinite number of equally successful theories differing from the former only by having wild predicates in them. Simplicity has to enter in to eliminate the background theories with the wild predicates, before it enters in to pick out theories of a new area which fit well with the non-eliminated theories.

18. See, for example, A. Pannekoek, *A History of Astronomy* (London: George Allen and Unwin, 1961), p. 303.

19. Boyd has claimed that judgements of projectability, that is, in effect simplicity in my sense, are judgements of 'theoretical plausibility' (that is, of fit with other existing theories), "where the determination of the relevant respects of resemblance is itself a theoretical issue," that is, that what constitutes 'fit' is in some way itself determined by the background. See Richard Boyd, "Realism, Approximate Truth and Philosophical Method," reprinted in ed. D. Papineau, *The Philosophy of Science* (Oxford: Oxford University Press, 1996), pp. 223-24. His view seems to arise from regarding background as consisting not merely of scientific theories in the ordinary sense but also of principles of inference, and this conglomeration of two very distinct things seems to arise from a claim that empirical data can provide evidence not merely for theories but for principles of inference. But these

principles of inference so established cannot be all the ones that there are—for then there would be no principles left in virtue of which the empirical data could provide evidence for them. Science must have some a priori contribution. If it is suggested that the procedure of establishing principles of inference is entirely circular, then there would be no reason for adopting one overall system of 'background knowledge' rather than any other—the coherentist's usual problem.

20. This is the answer to the objection of Colin Howson that use of the simplicity postulate is "at odds with reasonable procedures. In the case of hypotheses generated in economic forecasting, to take an extreme example, simple hypotheses would normally be regarded as very unlikely" ("On the Consistency of Jeffrey's Simplicity Postulate and its Role in Bayesian Inference," p. 78). But the reason why such hypotheses are very unlikely is that very simple hypotheses have worked poorly in the past in social and economic theory, while the simplest among hypotheses of a certain kind and degree of complexity have done better; and so a new hypothesis, to fit well with such hypotheses, will have to postulate the same kinds of complex interactions—in other words a new relatively complex hypothesis will make for a simpler overall theory than does a new very simple hypothesis.

21. I owe this point to Peter Lipton, "Is the Best Good Enough?" *Proceedings of the Aristotelian Society* 93 (1992/3), pp. 89-104. He infers—correctly—that

scepticism about the ability of science to give absolute rankings to the worth of theories must lead to scepticism about its ability to give comparative rankings.

22. Supposedly Archimedes formulated his law in his bath, Newton formulated his theory after watching an apple drop, and Einstein once worked in a patent office.

23. David Hume, *Treatise of Human Nature,* 1.3.6.

24. "How to Tell When Simpler, More Unified, and Less Ad Hoc Theories will Provide More Accurate Predictions," *British Journal for Philosophy of Science* 45 (1994), pp. 1-35.

25. If L and P do not fit the data equally well, a more complicated relation holds between how well they do fit the data (their "log-likelihood") and their (probable) predictive accuracy—see Forster and Sober, p.10.

26. See A. Kukla, "Forster and Sober on the Curve-Fitting Problem," *British Journal for the Philosophy of Science* 46 (1995), pp. 248-52.

27. See, for example, Pannekoek, *A History of Astronomy,* pp. 359-62.

THE AQUINAS LECTURES
Published by the Marquette University Press
Milwaukee WI 53201-1881 USA

About the Aquinas Lecture Series

The Annual St. Thomas Aquinas Lecture Series began at Marquette University in the Spring of 1937. Ideal for classroom use, library additions, or private collections, the Aquinas Lecture Series has received international acceptance by scholars, universities, and libraries. Hardbound in maroon cloth with gold stamped covers. Uniform style and price ($15 each). Some reprints with soft covers. Complete set (60 Titles) (ISBN 0-87462-150-X) receives a 40% discount. New standing orders receive a 30% discount. Regular reprinting keeps all volumes available. Ordering information (purchase orders, checks, and major credit cards accepted):

Bookmasters Distribution Services
1444 U.S. Route 42
Mansfield OH 44903
Order Toll-Free (800) 247-6553
FAX: (419) 281 6883
Editorial Address:
Dr. Andrew Tallon, Director
Marquette University Press
Box 1881
Milwaukee WI 53201-1881
Tel: (414) 288-7298 FAX: (414) 288-3300
Internet: tallona@vms.csd.mu.edu. CompuServe: 73627,1125
Web Page: http://www.mu.edu/mupress/

ISBN 0-87462-163-1

9 780874 621631